What Our Readers Have Said...

Applicability

"These books are great tools that should be used as guidelines for our everyday supervisory practices. You need to take the time to do a short self-evaluation when reading them."

•

"The Pinpoint Training Series delivers information that could be used in a lot different areas."

•

"The things and problems we deal with everyday are discussed in these books."

Convenience

"I like this because I can take them with me to read at a convenient time. I feel the little time I have to spend in the office is best use on activities that directly relate to revenue opportunities. I like the short amount of time it takes to keep up with these."

•

"I prefer the self-study approach; it fits in with my schedule."

•

"I like the fact that the format allows the books to be reviewed as time permits. All work has been conducted on personal, evening/weekend time."

•

"Easy to use... if you put the time into it."

Challenge

"My thought is that the real value of these books comes into effect when doing the action plans."

•

"I like the fact that the format allows assignments to be reviewed as time permits."

Clarity

"Short and sweet. These books are easy to comprehend."

•

"Easy to use, understand, and reference if needed."

Relevance

"I have enjoyed reading these books. They are relevant to today's work environment and the ongoing change in the way we manage our workforce."

•

"I believe the contents of the Pinpoint series are excellent. It causes one to reflect on the daily dynamics in working with oneself as well as with management and peers."

Resolving Conflict in the Workplace

Pinpoint Leadership Skill Development Training Series

TIMOTHY F. BEDNARZ

MAJORIUM
BUSINESS PRESS

Pinpoint Leadership Skill Development Training Series
"Resolving Conflict in the Workplace"
Timothy F. Bednarz

Graphic design: Monika Pawlak

Majorium Business Press
2025 Main Street
Stevens Point, WI 54481
715.342.1018 • 800.654.4935

ISBN 978-1-62101-046-3

Printed in the United States of America

Introduction

The Pinpoint Leadership Skill Development Training Series is designed for targeted training and education regarding increased improvement in a specific skill or competency.

Each book within this series is designed to be easy to use, understand and apply to your job. It can be used as a basis for training individuals, as a discussion guide or as a personal training tool.

Each chapter within this book discusses a specific concept. When you have completed all eight chapters you should have a 360° perspective of the topic.

Additionally, each chapter is divided into specific sections:

- The first section provides you with an overview of the topic
- The Implications section discusses why the concept is important, and why it is important to learn and apply.
- The Strategies, Tips & Techniques to Apply section teaches how to use and apply the particular concept to your work.
- The Points to Ponder section gives you something to think about or to be discussed with a group setting. These are questions not meant to be immediately answered, but to be pondered over time.
- The Training Activity section provides you with the tools to transfer what you have learned to your job. It is designed to help create an action plan to effectively apply the concept.

Each of the topics in this series is time-tested and proven in the marketplace. They have been used by thousands of employees as training tools. Many of the users have commented that what made these books valuable, was the ability to refer to them when a problem surfaced. They indicated that they remembered reading about the exact problem. They referred back to these books and found an appropriate solution.

You will find them equally valuable as a resource in your professional development library.

Table of Contents

LEARNING OBJECTIVES:

- To identify the critical factors and benefits of the conflict resolution process and the impact it has upon leadership.
- To understand the implications and ramifications that either enhance, or diminish conflict resolution and its functions and process.
- How to overcome the problems and pitfalls associated with the conflict resolution process.
- How to apply effective strategies to overcoming conflict.
- To understand cause and effect relationships and their impact as a result of failing to resolve conflict issues and situations.
- To apply strategies to effectively enhance one's ability to resolve conflict situations effectively.

1

Conflict Is More Than Simply "Not Getting Along"

The existence of conflict is commonplace within any organization. Whenever individuals of diverse interests and backgrounds interact with one another, conflict will arise. In some management circles, conflict is viewed negatively. However, when effective conflict resolution techniques are applied, productive agreements can be reached, solidifying personal relationships in a manner that makes the organization stronger.

IMPLICATIONS — WHAT THIS MEANS TO YOU

Conflicts should be considered part of the normal business environment. As leaders build teams consisting of diverse people with differing abilities, disagreements will arise. This diversity is what brings synergy and a sense of balance to the team.

The key to effective conflict resolution is to view it as an opportunity and not a sign that a problem exists within the organization. A team created with productive synergy brings many perspectives to the table. Conflict develops when these perspectives clash with one another; but this is the opportunity to stimulate a healthy debate around the issues and arrive at a consensus.

The problem leaders often encounter is that many individuals have an aversion to conflict and prefer to run from it, which confines these team members to a play-it-safe world where little is accomplished or learned. Conflicts are allowed to fester, resulting in long-term problems that will at some point need to be resolved.

STRATEGIES, TIPS & TECHNIQUES TO APPLY

When leaders encounter conflict within their organization, there are four critical factors they need to be aware of in order to reach a successful resolution. These factors are:

Attitude

While conflict is a healthy opportunity for an organization to grow, all parties involved must possess a positive attitude if the conflict is going to be resolved. If both parties don't want to arrive at a resolution, it won't happen until someone intervenes and forces the issue; and even so, the conflict can continue to fester if one or both parties feel the solution was forced upon them.

Personal Agendas

When conflict occurs, personality differences, personal agendas and feelings left over from past problems often arise and interfere with the resolution. Until all parties are willing to put these issues aside and look beyond them toward common issues and concerns, the conflict will continue. All concerned must ask themselves what is more important: clinging to their personal opinions and perceived injuries, or working together to solve a problem that is essential to the success of the organization and ultimately to each individual involved in the conflict?

Communication

Within the context of conflict resolution, true communication must take place, which requires active listening much more than just persuasively arguing for one point of view over another. Communicating entails listening to learn and appreciate the other party's needs and concerns. Before any successful resolution can transpire, all parties' concerns must be addressed. Effective communication is the key to effective leadership, management and organizational health.

Dedication to the Success of the Relationship

The leader's goal in conflict resolution must go beyond merely keeping the peace and averting a crisis: they must foster a productive relationship between the individuals involved in the conflict in order to build positive momentum. In order for this momentum to be strong and enduring, conflict resolution must be dedicated to the success of the relationship, and not to the fulfillment of one's wishes over another's. This process keeps all parties focused on what is good for the organization rather than on the advancement of their personal agendas and quest for power.

The key is to face the problem, separate the personalities involved, and then commit to resolving the matter in a way that meets all parties' needs. In this way, conflict develops into an opportunity for all parties to grow while advancing the organization.

POINTS TO PONDER — SOMETHING TO THINK ABOUT

1. How often do you see personal agendas and personality differences interfering with the ability to resolve a conflict?
2. Do you have a personal inclination to flee from conflict, or do you embrace it as an opportunity?

TRAINING ACTIVITY — APPLICATION & ACTION PLAN

Create a conflict scorecard that allows you to identify the key factors in a successful and effective conflict resolution. Use the four elements below as a checklist when dealing with future conflicts within your organization.

- Attitude
- Personal Agendas
- Communication
- Dedication to the Success of the Relationship

2

Types and Management of Conflict in the Workplace

Conflict takes many forms and has both positive and negative effects on an organization. A spirited debate around the issues in a group or team environment can involve friction but still be considered positive. More commonly though, conflict is associated with problems and arguments where the concerns are both negative and personal.

IMPLICATIONS — WHAT THIS MEANS TO YOU

The human factor must always be considered when dealing with teams. At all levels of the organization, people are struggling with three loaded questions in the group environment: Am I accepted by the group? Do I have value in the group? And do I have influence within the group? Since individual group members are seeking the answers to these questions, they can become sensitized to the situation and take healthy conflict and debate personally.

If conflict becomes a problem within a group the leader is heading, it is unlikely all viewpoints and perspectives will be voiced, heard and considered. Additionally, it is less likely that participants will share sensitive information or feel comfortable pointing out inconsistencies in other members' thinking.

STRATEGIES, TIPS & TECHNIQUES TO APPLY

An exploration of various forms of workplace conflict will help leaders understand both the benefits and consequences of tension and discord in the workplace. Even the absence of conflict has ramifications that leaders must understand. The following types of conflict are commonplace:

Task Conflict

A group's ability to engage in constructive conflict is vital to their cohesiveness and productivity. Simply stated, if leaders want to develop their working groups into effective teams, they need to facilitate the open airing of divergent outlooks and opinions. Group members must be able to embrace others' individual differences in order to take advantage of their talents. This type of collaboration allows members to create a collective identity in a constructive environment where conflict can be safely explored. To have a highly productive group, an honest, objective discussion of diverse points of view and a frank questioning of assumptions must occur. The result will be stronger and more creative decisions.

Groupthink

Some working groups suffer from a lack of task conflict. Within this groupthink environment, individual members voluntarily restrict their personal voicing of criticism and concerns regarding proposed ideas and courses of action. Because they cease to rigorously question and critique any of the proposals, they develop fewer objections. Leaders will see that the use of homogenous groups along with time pressures further increases the likelihood of developing groupthink.

When leaders encounter a groupthink environment, they can respond by assigning a group member to play the role of devil's advocate. Additionally, leaders should clearly demonstrate the value of constructive analysis by taking time to carefully explore the criticism of proposals and ideas. This practice is especially helpful when groups are minimizing or avoiding important problems.

Affective Conflict

Escalating task conflict can result in stress, strained emotions and tense relationships between group members, also known as affective or interpersonal conflict. Seldom constructive, affective conflict can quickly undermine the effectiveness of a group, leading individual members to use negative emotions to personalize substantive debates and develop cycles of negative attributions concerning the personal motives and capabilities of other group members.

It is essential that leaders not ignore the existence of affective conflict. Unfortunately, in many groups norms are in place allowing for only the expression of positive feelings or mild disagreement, to the exclusion of anger. However, as suppressing anger within the group only allows it to fester and surface at a later date, it is generally better for leaders to address these tendencies as quickly as possible. The longer anger remains unaddressed, the more prone it is to erupt in conflagration, rendering it difficult if not impossible for the group to discuss the underlying issues constructively.

Intervention

There are instances when levels of conflict have become so pronounced that effective communication is hindered. This is when leaders need to suspend the task discussion and have the group examine its own processes in an attempt to define and resolve the conflicts. Leaders can use the following techniques:

- Be clear in defining what is considered appropriate behavior among group members.
- Reinforce and support what is considered desirable behavior.
- Address inappropriate behavior when it occurs. In certain instances, a personal discussion with the offending group member may be called for. The discussion should be grounded in facts, minimizing their ability to personalize the issue.
- Generate several meaningful alternatives for the group to consider.
- Create a sense of fairness by empowering all group members.
- Ensure that all members share the group's goals. A great deal of conflict is rooted in disagreement over the direction of the group.

POINTS TO PONDER — SOMETHING TO THINK ABOUT

1. Were you aware of the various types of workplace conflict?
2. Do you see ways to productively harness conflict in your organization?

TRAINING ACTIVITY — APPLICATION & ACTION PLAN

1. As organizational conflict in some form is common, look at your work environment and identify which of the three forms normally develop:
    - Task Conflict
    - Groupthink
    - Affective Conflict
2. If problems generally arise in the latter two categories, identify the causes and develop plans to intervene in order to bring the situation within the boundaries of task conflict.

3

Conflict at Work

The particular style of problem solving and conflict resolution employed is the most important variable in determining group effectiveness. Research has further shown that the predominant mode of conflict resolution characterizing the leadership and management of groups is the most consistent determinant of a company's profitability.

IMPLICATIONS — WHAT THIS MEANS TO YOU

The manner in which leaders resolve problems and overcome conflict within their organizations may appear of little consequence as long as the problem is solved and conflict eliminated. However, leaders must understand the group dynamics impacting solutions and their consequences.

It is important for leaders to understand the complexity of workplace problem solving, and that, depending upon group norms and specific contexts, various modes of conflict resolution will come into play. In order to be consistently successful, leaders should recognize the various styles of conflict resolution that can be effective depending upon the circumstances and the makeup of the individuals involved in the conflict.

STRATEGIES, TIPS & TECHNIQUES TO APPLY

Leaders will encounter a variety of common conflict resolution modes in the workplace. These styles highlight prototypical approaches, with most groups acting in ways that contain one or more of these modes in their efforts to deal with conflict.

Smoothing and Avoiding

These groups tend to be comprised of accommodating individuals who, when a problem or conflict occurs, will tend to define it in a manner that minimizes the differences between individuals. Their objective is to maintain the status quo within the group. As a whole, this method of conflict resolution is destructive because it does not address the central issues or actually resolve the sources of conflict. Consequently, these issues tend to fester within the group and will emerge later as a larger problem.

The group norms that identify the smoothing and avoiding behavior include individuals who tend to withdraw when attacked in order to avoid conflict. Additionally, individual group members tend to keep their feelings and remarks in check so that they don't surface. This effectively masks internal conflict and prevents the leader, as well as the group, from identifying the undercurrents that are present.

Confronting and Problem Solving

This form of conflict resolution represents the healthiest behavior. The members of this group tend to be collaborators. They will define the problem relative to the total organization's needs versus their own. The outcomes of this group are interdependent if the total group benefits from the solution.

The group norms that identify the confronting and problem solving behavior include individuals who feel it is important to bring out and confront the differences of opinion and perspective within the group. They also feel that all solutions to conflict should be open and fair to all involved and to the organization as a whole. The group will tend to arrive at answers and solutions by reason rather than the application of personal power and authority.

Confronting and problem solving behaviors are generally the most effective mode for resolving group conflicts.

Bargaining and Forcing

This form of conflict resolution behavior favors and is beneficial to specific power groups and personal agendas. It takes a winning-at-all-costs slant that positions one group against another. The problems tend to be defined in terms of the stakes of each group. The participants and the atmosphere are confrontational and adversarial. The outcome favors one group at the expense of all others.

The group norms that typify bargaining and forcing behaviors include individuals who will seize the advantage whenever possible and compromise when the advantage is the other group's. Individuals will tend to maximize the benefits for themselves over the other individual members.

POINTS TO PONDER — SOMETHING TO THINK ABOUT

1. What conflict resolution mode have you seen most commonly used?
2. What conflict resolution mode do you feel is most appropriate in your work environment?

TRAINING ACTIVITY — APPLICATION & ACTION PLAN

Listed below are the three conflict resolution modes:

- Smoothing and Avoiding
- Confronting and Problem Solving
- Bargaining and Forcing

1. Identify situations where you have witnessed each of these modes in action.
2. Identify the outcomes and consequences of each of these modes.
3. Determine what mode is most effective in your workplace.

4

Pitfalls and Problems Associated with Conflict Resolution Outcomes in the Workplace

Conflict resolution and problem solving are most often conducted within group settings under a leader's direction. Though groups have the potential to produce highly effective and innovative solutions, many have behavioral patterns that make it difficult for them to reach their potential.

IMPLICATIONS — WHAT THIS MEANS TO YOU

There are many organizational settings that restrict the leader's ability to resolve conflicts and problems on an individual basis. Most have no option but to bring these issues to a group setting, whether it be a standing committee or regular staff meeting. In these settings, leaders must understand not only the group dynamics that impact decision making and problem solving, but also the common problems that can befall groups and affect their effectiveness and productivity.

It is important for leaders to understand that an awareness of group problems allows for keen observation and the ability to overcome pitfalls before they further complicate the process and undermine the group.

More importantly, each group creates a synergy where the group is greater than the sum total of its individual parts. Pitfalls that affect groups also impact its synergy. Such problems can create biases and slants that adversely influence results and outcomes, even without the conscious knowledge of the members.

STRATEGIES, TIPS & TECHNIQUES TO APPLY

There are a number of complicated issues leaders need to watch for when resolving conflict in a group setting.

Differences in Problem Solving Styles

Individuals tend to develop fixed patterns of thinking that affect their perspective. Engineers and accountants tend to rely on quantitative techniques, while architects and designers will use pictures and diagrams to frame the problem. Others rely on feelings and intuition. Often these set thinking patterns prevent individuals from stepping outside of their box to objectively view other perspectives and viewpoints. Rather than simplify the solution process, this can create additional sources of conflict.

More Knowledge and Information

Individuals bring varied levels of knowledge, expertise and information to a group setting. This can be used to the group's advantage if the leader can apply the diversity of knowledge, skills and thinking to the search for innovative solutions. However, if the group is confrontational and adversarial, one set of individuals can use their knowledge and information to gain an advantage over other members.

Use of Organizational Resources

Group decision making clearly consumes more time and organizational resources than individual decision making. If the process is efficient and effective, the payoff is relative to the investment. However, groups can tend to draw out the process and consume more resources than necessary to arrive at a solution and consensus among individual members.

Pressure to Conform

The pressure to conform can be dangerous in groups where individual members differ in their levels of authority, status and power. Within these settings it is especially difficult for less influential people to confront the opinions of more powerful members or disagree with them.

In other settings, conformity to the group becomes an important criterion for being accepted and belonging. In either circumstance, diversity of viewpoints and an open discussion of the issues are hampered. These results impact the quality of problem solving, decisions and overall group efforts.

Personal Agendas

The most common pitfall and problem associated with conflict resolution and group problem solving is the propensity of individuals or small coalitions to aggressively advance a personal viewpoint or agenda in an effort to seize control. The process deteriorates into a situation where winning is more important than arriving at a proper and appropriate decision.

As discussions focus on substantive issues, deeper levels of debate will often involve undercurrents of power, prestige and influence. When specific parties perceive an attack on their personal position and authority, they will often argue the loudest to protect that position.

Riskier Decisions

Individual members can frequently lose their individual identity and sense of responsibility. Solutions are usually arrived at by combining several recommendations and by obtaining a group consensus. Research does show that this often produces riskier solutions than those any of its members would have agreed to individually. Consequently, poorer decisions can be arrived at that individual members can also then deny personal responsibility for.

Solution Orientation

In many group settings, the group will tend to focus on the solution, short-circuiting the analysis process needed to effectively define the problem and the parameters of the solution. This process tends to focus on symptoms without examining and understanding root causes. The nature of the issue is inadequately explored and the solution is insufficient to resolve the problem and the conflict.

POINTS TO PONDER — SOMETHING TO THINK ABOUT

1. What are the most common problems and pitfalls you encounter in conflict resolution?
2. What frustrates you the most in resolving problems and conflicts in a group setting?

TRAINING ACTIVITY — APPLICATION & ACTION PLAN

Identify the pitfalls and problems associated with conflict resolution and problem solving that you have experienced.

- Differences in Problem Solving Styles
- More Knowledge and Information
- Use of Organizational Resources
- Pressure to Conform
- Personal Agendas
- Riskier Decisions
- Solution Orientation

1. Pinpoint the specific problems that most commonly occur.
2. Identify the specifics of each of these common problems.
3. Determine which actions can be undertaken to eliminate these individual problems and pitfalls.

5

The Right Conflict Resolution Strategies Make Leadership Easier

Organizations and their leaders face daily a number of situations and circumstances where effective conflict resolution styles must be brought to bear in order to enact the best solution for the organization and its people. This process goes beyond compromise and consensus to an exploration of how problems are defined and which group norms are best to use.

IMPLICATIONS — WHAT THIS MEANS TO YOU

Conflict in the workplace isn't limited to personal differences between one or more employees. It includes the ability of different groups and departments within the organization to create effective solutions to various problems, such as the allocation of limited resources or the priority of specific projects and agendas within the company. Within this environment, individuals and groups bring various degrees of conflict resolution skills and styles to the table.

STRATEGIES, TIPS & TECHNIQUES TO APPLY

The complexity of conflict resolution includes a variety of tactics and styles used in the process, even those used by unskilled and untrained employees. In LLD-036, three styles of conflict resolution were discussed:

Smoothing & Avoiding

This style is used to minimize differences between group members and maintain the status quo.

Confronting and Problem Solving

This style is used to define the problem relative to the total needs of the organization and to create an interdependent solution.

Bargaining and Forcing

This style is used to define the problem in terms of the stakes for each subgroup and to create a win/lose outcome.

Comparison of the Three Styles

As noted in the previous lesson, these are typical definitions of conflict resolution styles. While most groups evidence a predominant method, many will operate using elements from some or all of these styles. It should be noted that each group's unique mixture of styles can vary over time depending on the type of problem at hand.

The confronting and problem solving style is considered to be the most effective in getting individuals to collaborate and resolve conflicts. However, there are circumstances where the smoothing and avoiding style or bargaining and forcing may be a more appropriate way to resolve conflicts.

Invariably, there are situations where significant time pressures may force a group to arrive at a decision without fully exploring the individual needs and positions of the members. In these circumstances, leaders may have no alternative other than to suppress internal group conflict in the interest of arriving at a timely decision. However, this can create a dangerous precedent, as there is a pronounced difference between the utilization of a one-time, short-term strategy to meet a deadline and the longer-term development of group norms that actively and repeatedly suppress conflict. The danger is that successive short-term crises will justify a smoothing and avoiding approach in the group, with often only a few crises needed to create a long-term pattern.

The bargaining and forcing resolution style is probably the most common form of conflict resolution. While it may not be the most effective, it is often applied where two or more groups or departments within the organization are vying for scarce resources. In the absence of clear organizational priorities, bargaining and forcing is the only way to resolve such interdepartmental conflict.

Additionally, bargaining and forcing can be a particularly useful approach with groups that meet infrequently and individual members who don't know each other well, or when the organization does not have a clear sense of direction.

The problems associated with bargaining and forcing are that the climate often quickly degenerates into the use of confrontational tactics. The goal of winning takes priority over arriving at the best solution. The interests of the group are subverted by the quest for scarce resources or prominence.

Under these circumstances, the confronting and problem solving style is highly desirable. However, this tack requires that participants possess the analytical and interpersonal skills to create an open discussion of important differences within the group. These groups have the ability to handle the stress of disagreement as well as the necessary tools to deal with tension and solve problems.

POINTS TO PONDER — SOMETHING TO THINK ABOUT

1. How would you define the predominant resolution style within your organizational unit?
2. What other styles are incorporated with it?

TRAINING ACTIVITY — APPLICATION & ACTION PLAN

Define three or more conflict situations you were recently or are currently involved with.

1. Define the problem according to the three conflict styles listed above.
2. Identify the potential outcomes using each style.
3. Compare and contrast in order to arrive at the best style for the problem.

6

The High Price of Conflict in the Workplace

While internal conflict and friction can be healthy for an organization in that it can channel that energy into creative and innovative solutions, there are times when leaders must understand that conflict can be costly, especially if personal interests and agendas are placed above the needs of the organization.

IMPLICATIONS — WHAT THIS MEANS TO YOU

Inherent in any conflict is the base struggle for survival. It may be the survival of one's point of view, perspective or power base. In other instances, it may be the struggle of one group or department over another. In all cases, this struggle must be recognized and balanced against the needs of the organization.

By definition, leaders are concerned with the entire organization, not just their own personal spheres of influence. Leaders must rise above the desire to attain a power base or advance an agenda. They must direct any conflict resolution toward creating and crafting the best possible solution for the entire organization.

STRATEGIES, TIPS & TECHNIQUES TO APPLY

While conflict is healthy in most working environments, there are two general areas where conflict can be damaging and destructive to the entire organization.

Personal Agendas and Perspectives

One of the most problematic areas of conflict resolution is the application of personal agendas and perspectives to conflict resolution. A natural tendency in all individuals, this can cause difficulties if the personal agenda of one or more members of a group overpower the needs of the organization. This is especially problematic when someone senior to the rest of the group members is advancing the personal agenda. The areas where individual personal agendas can be damaging include:

Biased assimilation of information – How a problem or conflict is perceived and defined impacts its resolution. Personal agendas and perceptions can create a bias that adversely affects the definition of the problem and ultimately, the solution. This misstep occurs when information and data is received from an external source and processed with a lack of understanding or adequate background information. Additionally, the information can be processed using incorrect assumptions, perceptions or decision making norms to frame the issue; this ultimately impacts the formation of the solution in regard to conclusions and the actions caused by them.

When personal agendas strongly influence a group—either in the form of intimidation or by the use of power over the group—there is a reluctance to question the information and perspectives being presented. The group assumes a smoothing and avoiding conflict resolution style that allows these differences in opinion and perspective to be both minimized and glossed over. When a wrong decision is made that impacts the organization, the primary influencer can disclaim any exclusive association by pointing out the group nature of the decision. This tactic serves to mask any personal agenda at play, often to extremely destructive effect.

Partisan perceptions – Research has demonstrated that there is an unconscious tendency in individuals to enhance their own side of a conflict, portraying it as more insightful, honest and morally upright. An associated phenomenon is the tendency to vilify the opposition, portraying them as both unscrupulous and vile. These two phenomena have dominated research on inter-group relations for over 40 years. In more recent studies, the insidious and involuntary nature of partisan tactics has become more apparent as it affects the nature of conflict and the specific manners in which the resolution process is undermined.

When applied to the aforementioned concept of biased assimilation of information, it is obvious how conflict intensifies when one group strongly believes in their viewpoints while simultaneously vilifying their opponents'. Organizations feel the impact as the conflict degenerates into personal battles and animosities that can endure for prolonged periods of time. This partisanship poisons the workplace environment to the point that satisfactory resolution becomes nearly impossible without outside intervention.

Scarce Resources

The other major source of internal conflict within organizations is the battle between groups and departments over the utilization of limited resources. This situation readily surfaces when organizations lack clear direction.

In certain circumstances, larger and more powerful departments are able to dominate this battle and intimidate smaller and less influential groups. While this "survival of the fittest" confrontation might be considered productive by some members of management, it is ultimately unhealthy and damaging if badly needed resources are diverted away from those areas of the organization most in need of them or from those who can put them to the most productive use.

POINTS TO PONDER — SOMETHING TO THINK ABOUT

1. What is the nature of most of the conflict you've observed in your organization?
2. What effect and impact has conflict had in your workplace over the past several years?

TRAINING ACTIVITY — APPLICATION & ACTION PLAN

1. Identify three or four sources of conflict that have provided positive benefits to the organization.
2. Identify three or four sources of conflict that have been detrimental to the organization.
3. Compare and contrast both groups to understand how and why the consequences resulted in either a positive or negative impact.
4. Determine what lessons can be learned through this analysis.

7

Conflict Turns Effective Leadership Decision Making Upside Down

Conflict and problems do not typically occur in a vacuum. The roots of existing conflict reside within each organization and its individual members. These potential conflicts can undermine the leader's ability to direct the group and make sound decisions that result in a positive outcome.

IMPLICATIONS — WHAT THIS MEANS TO YOU

Leaders are confronted with a dilemma when it comes to conflict resolution. If they are unable to find the most workable fit between the problems that result in conflict and the group they direct, their ability to lead their employees will be diminished.

Many of the factors that lead to conflict and undermine a leader's ability can be treated independently. Conflict resolution is complex, and leaders must identify contributing factors and modify their approach accordingly in order to arrive at the best solution. This takes time, attention to detail, and a careful assessment of the most critical elements and surrounding circumstances within each specific conflict situation.

STRATEGIES, TIPS & TECHNIQUES TO APPLY

Not all leaders are in situations where their people possess sophisticated interpersonal skills and have an open mind toward the resolution of conflict. In fact, many manage and direct groups whose makeup creates additional conflict rather than solutions to already existing situations. This places leaders at a disadvantage and creates situations where their ability to lead is undermined.

Leaders should be cognizant of the following workplace factors and circumstances that can lead to a diminishing of management capabilities.

Required Knowledge and Analytical Skills

Conflict takes many forms from simple arguments between employees over minor issues to more sophisticated discussions and negotiations regarding issues of unit efficiency and productivity. Yet no matter the type of conflict, without required group knowledge and analytical skills to evaluate the problem and arrive at an objective assessment, problems will occur. Groups will assume a predominantly smoothing and avoiding approach to maintain the status quo or a bargaining and forcing mode that is destructive to the cohesiveness of the group and the organization. Both modes consistently applied in all circumstances will erode the leader's ability to lead and direct their organization.

If leaders observe some of their people lacking the requisite skills and knowledge to effectively deal with conflict within the group, they must determine whether they have the capacity, and if so, take the necessary actions to ensure this aptitude is acquired. In this fashion, leaders can transform potentially dangerous situations into ones that enhance their ability to lead.

Workloads

Groups can have the required knowledge and analytical skills to effectively handle internal conflict, but be so overburdened with other tasks and responsibilities that their ability to work through it is still greatly diminished. The constraints of other higher priority assignments lessen both the desire and ability of members to manage their conflicts. As such clashes are viewed as an unnecessary interruption in more important work, they defer resolution to the leader.

High levels of stress generally characterize overloaded groups. High stress leads to shallow and incomplete diagnosis as well as a preference for solutions that are simple and inflexible rather than creative and effective.

Expectations

Each individual member of a group has an established idea regarding the degree to which they will become involved in conflict resolution. While approaches vary according to participants' makeup and personality styles, the predominant mode of conflict resolution is smoothing and avoiding, where peace and the status quo are maintained. In other situations, depending upon company norms, some groups feel very strongly about their right to be involved in a decision. Research has shown that many of the tensions that develop between leaders and employees stem from differing assumptions regarding the appropriate degree of group participation in certain types of decisions.

Leaders must account for members' individual personality styles and expectations since reactions and expectations will vary from group to group.

Conflict Resolution Norms

Group conflict resolution can be especially difficult when individual members have different and/or conflicting goals and needs. The most critical aspect of a group's problem solving ability is its capacity to handle internal conflict. Leaders must ensure that the groups they direct have developed positive and healthy norms. Only when this is achieved is an appropriate forum created in which to work out problems and resolve conflict. Without these resolution norms, serious and heated group controversy will be divisive and result in ineffective and potentially harmful solutions.

POINTS TO PONDER — SOMETHING TO THINK ABOUT

1. Which aspects of conflict most negatively impact your ability to manage effectively?
2. What do you feel is the biggest weakness in your group regarding conflict resolution?

TRAINING ACTIVITY — APPLICATION & ACTION PLAN

The best offense is a good defense. While conflict continually occurs in the workplace, leaders should analyze the factors that can potentially diminish the ability to lead. They should review the following factors:

- Required Knowledge and Analytical Skills
- Workloads
- Expectations
- Conflict Resolution Norms

1. Evaluate the organizational unit against each of these factors.
2. Identify areas of potential problems and weaknesses.
3. Determine the factors needing strengthening or revising.
4. Implement or introduce the appropriate training or remedial actions.

8

Resolving Conflict Paves the Way to Higher Levels of Leadership Effectiveness

The natural tendencies of many individuals and other group dynamics can hinder a leader's ability to be effective in resolving conflict in the group setting. The leader must take the time to observe and then rectify specific behaviors that interfere with conflict resolution.

IMPLICATIONS — WHAT THIS MEANS TO YOU

When problems and issues arise, many individuals have a natural tendency to avoid friction. When that is not possible, they seek to remain uninvolved in its resolution. Employees may be forced to be part of a group charged with solving a problem, but these individuals are often not happy about it. The fight-or-flight response takes over, and even if they are physically present, they have mentally left the conflict.

When problems do occur leaders must ensure that all viewpoints and perspectives are heard and all alternatives explored. Techniques can be utilized to ensure that all members of the group are included in both the discussion and crafting of an acceptable solution.

STRATEGIES, TIPS & TECHNIQUES TO APPLY

Leaders can look for specific behavior patterns in order to determine how employees handle conflict. These patterns may be nonverbal and not readily apparent, but a careful examination will help leaders spotlight the behaviors impeding conflict resolution and enable them to address and rectify the situation. Such an examination includes looking at:

Alternatives

The first behavioral patterns leaders need to explore are the alternatives that are considered when solving a problem in the group setting. Problems can present themselves and additional conflicts can be created if employees tend to consider only a few potential alternatives. If leaders observe these patterns, they must engage the group in brainstorming techniques that explore all possible avenues toward resolution. This action fosters creative thinking within the group and provides innovative solutions to eliminate the causes of conflict.

Emphasis

Within some groups, the smoothing and avoiding approach to conflict resolution is predominant, resulting in areas of agreement being overemphasized while leaving areas of disagreement unexplored. This deficiency allows the situation to fester and explode into a bigger problem down the road. When leaders observe this pattern, they must shift the group's emphasis to balance areas of agreement with disagreement. All aspects must be fully examined and the alternatives considered before the problem can be adequately resolved.

Disagreement

Leaders need to observe how members respect individual disagreement, as group norms may keep any discordance from being voiced. In other situations, individuals who convey disagreement may be ridiculed, bullied or intimidated so that it is not taken seriously or considered by the group.

Leaders must ensure that all members of the group have an open and equal opportunity to voice any problems they might have and offer valid points and perspectives. Any attempt to quiet opposition will create additional conflict and deeper problems.

Agreement

There are many criteria that a group can consider in establishing agreement among its members. Some will use a majority vote, while others will arrive at a consensus before moving forward. Some group norms interpret a lack of opposition as agreement.

Leaders should shift the group toward a consensus where all viewpoints are both voiced and considered. All members of the group must be included, especially those who may be reluctant to say anything. Only in this fashion will all viewpoints, options or alternatives be considered.

Openness

In several conflict resolution modes, leaders should be watchful for members "stumping" for a specific viewpoint or perspective rather than inquiring about the potential alternatives available to the group.

Additionally, leaders can observe how actively members listen to each other's perspectives and whether or not the members respect the input of all individuals. These clues help the leader determine the group's openness to alternative perspectives.

Leaders must ensure that all perspectives are voiced and respected. The advocacy of one point of view without a full exploration of the facts and all possible solutions should not be tolerated.

Participation

The participation of individual members, their reactions to the group setting, and their involvement with specific issues should be carefully observed. Leaders should pay attention to whether members are apathetic, frustrated, defensive, warm or enthusiastic. Each of these emotional states will impact both conflict resolution and problem solving. Apathy, frustration and defensive postures can result in faulty or unresolved solutions that will lead to subsequent issues.

Leaders should meet with each employee displaying negative personal attributes in order to determine the causes of their attitudes. In some cases, these attributes can surface because conflict and disagreement are not tolerated. Individuals may feel that their opinions are not respected or wanted. Such difficulties must be addressed if the group is to be effective.

Interaction

The final area that leaders must monitor closely is the interaction of individual members within the group environment. Some of these factors have already been discussed, including individuals who are overly nice and polite and emote only positive feelings. Group members might too readily agree with one another while suppressing their true thoughts. This indicates that the group is in a destructive conflict resolution mode where suppression dominates and the status quo is maintained.

Leaders who observe these clues must intervene in meetings and take the initiative in order to draw out the true feelings and perspectives of the group. They can effectively do this by using open-ended questions that operate until satisfactory responses are obtained.

POINTS TO PONDER — SOMETHING TO THINK ABOUT

1. How well do your employees handle and resolve conflict in the group setting?
2. Do you feel that the group's actions tend to hinder your personal effectiveness?

TRAINING ACTIVITY — APPLICATION & ACTION PLAN

Over the next 30 days, observe the behavioral patterns of the individual members of the group you direct using the guidelines listed in this lesson. Do not take immediate action to rectify the behavior unless it is harmful. After 30 days and several meetings and discussions, you should have a good understanding of the dynamics of the group and how it approaches both conflict resolution and problem solving. Based upon your observations, take specific action to ensure that the group becomes effective in these techniques.

About the Author

Timothy F. Bednarz, Ph.D. is CEO of the American Management Development Group, Inc. For over 20 years he has researched, designed and authored hundreds of learning and development programs used by Fortune 1000 companies.

He is also the author of *Great! What Makes Leaders Great. What They Did, How They Did It and What You Can Learn from It* (2011).

Speaking Availability

Timothy F. Bednarz, Ph.D. is available for speaking engagements for your next meeting or association event. He can be contacted at 800-654-4935 or by e-mail at timothy.bednarz@majorium.com.

Bulk Sales

Bulk sales of this book or any other titles available from Majorium Business Press. Inquiries can be directed to sales@majorium.com, or by phone at 800-6654-4935.

Quick Order Form

Fax orders: 715-342-1118. Send this form.

Telephone orders: Call 800-654-4935 toll-free. Have your credit card ready.

Email orders: sales@majorium.com

Postal orders: Majorium Business Press, 2025 Main Street, Stevens Point, WI 54481, USA.

Please send the following books:

____

____

____

____

Please send more FREE information on:

❑Catalog ❑Speaking/Seminars ❑Mailing Lists ❑Consulting

Name: ____

Address: _______________________________________

City: ____________________ State: _____ Zip: __________

Telephone: _____________________________________

Email address: __________________________________

Sales tax: Please add 5.5% for products shipped to Wisconsin addresses.

Shipping by air:

United States: $4.00 for first book and $2.00 for each additional product.

International: $9.00 for first book; $5.00 for each additional product (estimate).

24542683R00027

Made in the USA
Lexington, KY
22 July 2013